NATIVE ESTATES:
RECORDS OF MOBILITY ACROSS
COLONIAL BOUNDARIES

Ellen Ndeshi Namhila

**NATIVE ESTATES:
RECORDS OF MOBILITY ACROSS
COLONIAL BOUNDARIES**

Carl Schlettwein Lecture 10
Basler Afrika Bibliographien

© 2017 The authors
© 2017 Basler Afrika Bibliographien

Basler Afrika Bibliographien
Namibia Resource Centre & Southern Africa Library
Klosterberg 23
P. O. Box
CH 4051 Basel
Switzerland
www.baslerafrika.ch

The Basler Afrika Bibliographien is part of the Carl Schlettwein Foundation

All rights reserved.
Cover image: Estate file of Tshombiri (Jombili) Amutenya yaKanipembe. Cover with wristband for contract workers' identification number found in the National Archives of Namibia. Reference number: NAW [47] Estates 1929, No. 15/1929 (picture: Werner Hillebrecht 2014).
Editors: Dag Henrichsen, Caroline Jeannerat
Layout and typesetting: Tilo Richter

ISBN 9783905758900
ISSN 22977058

FOREWORD

African social history thrives in many ways on the passionate inclination by scholars to provide ordinary people with a "voice" and "experience", as does much of social history in general. We read archives along and against the grain; we define "gaps" and go to great lengths to explain these and how to work around them. We are critical of master narratives and of concepts as transmitted through and mediated by the archives, and we are critical of the very notions of "voice" and "experience". The archival turn has led us to reflect on the epistemic frameworks which underpin any archive or collection and which always mediate and often condition—and (re-)define—the history of people about whom we write in the first instance. We de- and re-construct and then suggest a different, more nuanced or even new reading of archives, documents and narratives. We present discoveries from the archives and weave these into ambivalent, ruptured and always complex histories. These we regard as "incomplete" and surely fractured and limited histories.

A general public might have other aspirations when turning to historical narratives and/or seeking out an archive. As Ellen Ndeshi Namhila—writer, scholar and policy-maker in the fields of Namibian libraries, archives, heritage and historical research—has shown in her various publications, the general, non-scholarly public is indeed often interested in "voices" and "experiences". Her research is rooted in current public history debates, interests and demands and has led her to research and publish "voices" and narratives of marginalised men and women, of people marginalised by, in part, master narratives of the liberation movements.

In this lecture, she explains how current, postcolonial public needs and expectations for specific archival services—genealogical data and personal information of all sorts—led her into investigations of the epistemic foundations of the colonial records at the National Archives of Namibia. Her project became, in part, a research project on the history of that colonial and apartheid state's archives. Her research also targeted the archive of the National Archives—that particular site where the production and destruction of history and the resurrection and silencing of people and their pasts is, at least in theory, accounted for by archivists, and where the decision-making processes of the latter are, ideally speaking, documented.

Here, she summarises her findings on the disturbing history of the lives and deaths of files of a particular group of records—estate records. She firstly presents us with the racialized *social biography of files,* fonds, collections, finding aids and databases of the colonial state archive in order to find explanations for the postcolonial public service failures of the National Archives of Namibia. By doing so she, secondly, presents us with, indeed, "voices" and "experiences" as mediated through the so-called Native Estate records, these having been either lost, neglected, ignored or destroyed. Namhila opens the files she eventually does find and suggests, in a true spirit of discovery, numerous new research questions and topics for Southern African history. Yet she does so without losing sight of what is at stake beyond these questions and topics: biographical data and personal information about deceased colonial subjects that are relevant for and often very crucial to their postcolonial relatives and heirs. Her case study of the social biography of records, and the glimpses she provides from the contents of their files on the social history of ordinary African people, link archives and social history with the demands of a postcolonial audience other than that of researchers and scholars. Her study, which will also be published in its comprehensive form by the Basler Afrika Bibliographien, is once again a passionate statement on the power of producing and silencing pasts and histories.

Basel, 12 December 2016
Dag Henrichsen
Basler Afrika Bibliographien

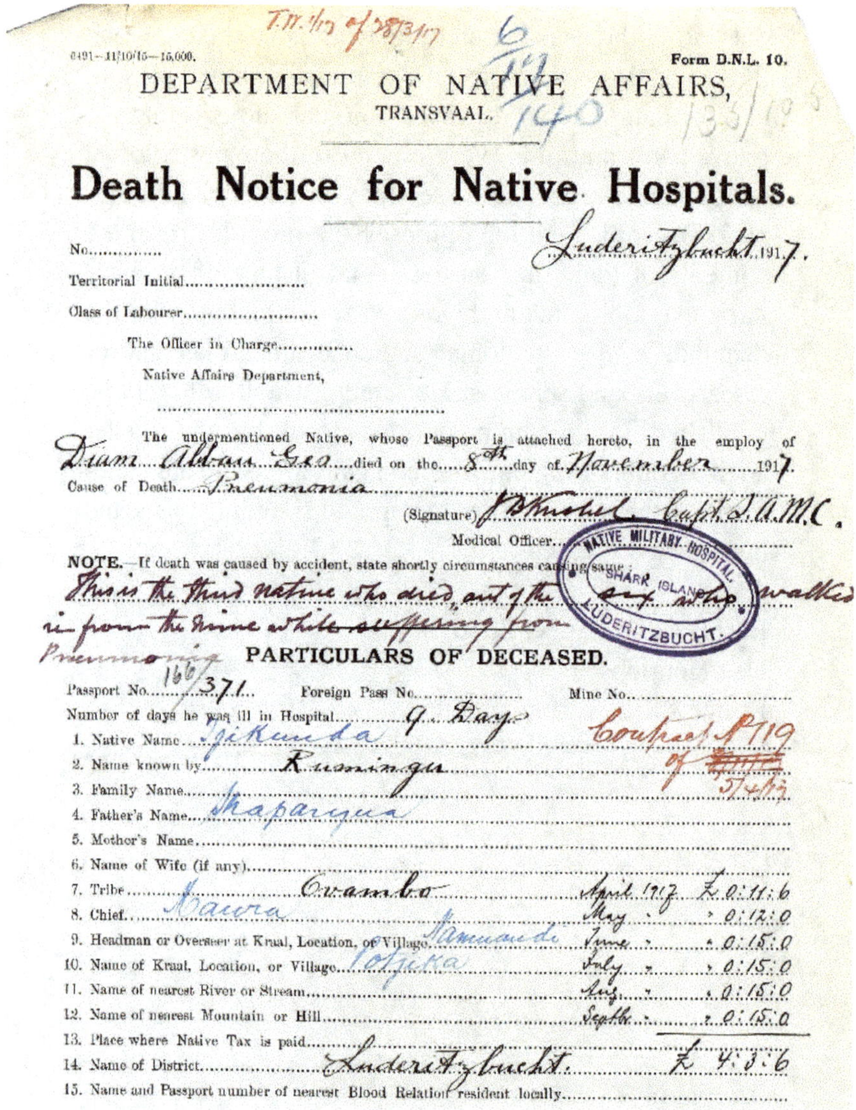

T.M. 1/13 of 28/3/17 6/74 140 135/105

6491—11/10/15—15,000. Form D.N.L. 10.

DEPARTMENT OF NATIVE AFFAIRS,
TRANSVAAL.

Death Notice for Native Hospitals.

No............... Luderitzbucht 1917.

Territorial Initial.......................

Class of Labourer.........................

The Officer in Charge..............

Native Affairs Department,

....

The undermentioned Native, whose Passport is attached hereto, in the employ of Diam Albau Geo died on the 8th day of November 1917.

Cause of Death Pneumonia

(Signature) J Knobel Capt. S.A.M.C.

Medical Officer.

NATIVE MILITARY HOSPITAL SHARK ISLAND LÜDERITZBUCHT.

NOTE.—If death was caused by accident, state shortly circumstances causing same: This is the third native who died, out of the six who walked in from the mine while suffering from Pneumonia

PARTICULARS OF DECEASED.

Passport No. 166/371 Foreign Pass No.................. Mine No..................

Number of days he was ill in Hospital 9 Days

1. Native Name Ijikumba Contract № 119 of 5/4/17
2. Name known by Rumingu
3. Family Name
4. Father's Name Shapangua
5. Mother's Name
6. Name of Wife (if any)
7. Tribe Ovambo April 1917 £ 0:11:6
8. Chief Nawra May " 0:12:0
9. Headman or Overseer at Kraal, Location, or Village Nammandi June " 0:15:0
10. Name of Kraal, Location, or Village Otjeka July " 0:15:0
11. Name of nearest River or Stream Aug " 0:15:0
12. Name of nearest Mountain or Hill Septbr " 0:15:0
13. Place where Native Tax is paid
14. Name of District Luderitzbucht £ 4:3:6
15. Name and Passport number of nearest Blood Relation resident locally

Figure 1: "This is the third native who died, out of the six who walked in from the mine while suffering from pneumonia."
(NAN NES [1] 135/105 Estate Rumingu)

NATIVE ESTATES: RECORDS OF MOBILITY ACROSS COLONIAL BOUNDARIES

I am greatly honoured to have been invited by the Centre for African Studies of the University of Basel to present the Carl Schlettwein Lecture 2015.

I count myself as very fortunate to have met Carl Schlettwein. In August 1998 the Basler Afrika Bibliographien (BAB) invited me to Basel for the first time to give a talk, following the publication of my first book, *The Price of Freedom*.[1] It was the beginning of a fruitful cooperation in which the Carl Schlettwein Foundation and the BAB enabled me to continue collecting oral history and writing the biography of the Namibian liberation struggle icon and Robben Island prisoner Eliaser Tuhadeleni, better known as Kaxumba Kandola. The BAB published the biography in 2005.[2]

Carl Schlettwein had lived in Namibia for a couple of years and fell in love with the country and its people. When he married Daniela Gsell, he settled in Switzerland. He once told me: "I could not live and raise my children in Namibia under apartheid, I did not want them to grow up as racists." It was in this spirit that he set up the BAB and the Carl Schlettwein Foundation as a resource for all humankind, irrespective of imagined boundaries of race and political ideology. The world is a better place because of people like Carl Schlettwein.

I sincerely thank the Centre for African Studies for inviting me to present this lecture. I hope it can stimulate some further research into forgotten and neglected historical sources.

Recently, I was able to defend my PhD-thesis at the University of Tampere, Finland, entitled *Recordkeeping and Missing "Native Estate" Records in Namibia: An Investigation of Colonial Gaps in a Post-Colonial National Archive*. I shall briefly refer to this research, as it provides the context for today's topic.

The motivation for my PhD research topic originated from problems in the user services of the National Archives of Namibia (NAN) during the time I served as its director (1999–2005) as they were reported to me by both its users and its staff.

The challenge was that many requests by black Namibians for pre-independence person-related civic records—such as adoption, divorce, or deceased estate files—could not be served by the Archives. Similar records requested by white Namibians were easily retrieved and served to clients within minutes. I selected estate records as the focus of my research because they were the most frequently requested files.

Estate files are legal records that are created after the death of a person to assist with administering the inheritance of the deceased's possessions in accordance with legal provisions and the wishes of the deceased. They are important documents that might have to be consulted over time to clarify property issues, for example after the death of a surviving spouse. But they

Figure 2: Estate records in the National Archives of Namibia—exclusively for white persons. (photo: Ellen Ndeshi Namhila)

are also very important documents for genealogists and family researchers as they supply not only information about the person himself or herself, such as the date and circumstances of death, but also about family connections.

The manual and electronic finding aids of the NAN allow the retrieval of estate files. When inspecting the shelves at the NAN, one finds rows over impressive rows of well-maintained and bound volumes with estate case files, labelled "EST" (see Figure 2).

However, a systematic examination of these files revealed that they all deal strictly with estates matters of white persons. Nothing could be found on estates of black persons or "Natives", as they used to be called. It seemed obvious to blame this fact on colonialism and apartheid. Namibia had been a German colony from 1884 to 1915, and then a South African colony until its independence on 21 March 1990. During that time it was administered by racially discriminatory laws and practices. But what was the procedure when black people died under apartheid and colonial rule? Were their estates not registered? Were no files created and maintained? Or were they destroyed? Why could they not be found in the NAN when requested by users?

I researched the archival and historical literature to establish whether this disparity is a widespread colonial phenomenon or only confined to Namibia, possibly due to the peculiarity of its records that originate from the entangled structures of colonialism and apartheid. A study of the literature revealed, however, that the issue of why and how the colonial situation affected the content and accessibility of archival material concerning person-related records for colonised peoples had not been investigated at all.

This research gap inspired me to conduct an in-depth exploration into the colonial records at the NAN, using deceased estate records of black Namibians—"Native Estates" as they had been called—as a case study.

I also investigated the legal environment, executive structures and administrative processes of estate record creation and management, disposal and transfer, as well as the continual custodianship of such records after their transfer to the National Archives. As such I examined their listing and appraisal, destruction or processing, indexing and metadata enhancement, in order to explain their apparent absence from the Archives. During these explorations I unexpectedly stumbled across a major research resource, some 11 250 Native Estates records, most of them hitherto unlisted.

LEGAL BACKGROUND

A first research question on the legal background of the Native Estates files had to look into two different sets of legislation: German (colonial) laws applicable in Namibia between 1884 and 1915, and South African laws applicable from 1915 to 1990.

The German law of inheritance was regulated by the German Civil Code ("Bürgerliches Gesetzbuch") of 1890, which did not prescribe any discrimination according to race. German colonialism was originally based on so-called "protection treaties" with indigenous communities, in which legal matters among the members of the colonised communities were not considered to fall under the jurisdiction of German courts. Therefore one could not expect any Native Estates files in the early German colonial records.

This changed with the colonial war of 1904 to 1908 when protection treaties were nullified and all legal matters in German South West Africa fell under the German authorities. However, as the German colonial government expropriated all land and cattle from the "Natives", they were basically left with no property to be inherited.

When the South African armed forces occupied the territory in 1915, they brought along their legislation that was already racially discriminating. Section 3 (1) (d) of the "Administration of Estate Act, No. 24 of 1913", which was made applicable in South West Africa, specifically excluded "Native" estates. These remained unregulated until 1928 when the separate "Native Administration Proclamation No. 15 of 1928" was promulgated.

There are two crucial differences between the two sets of legislation:

White estates, on the one hand, were governed by the "Administration of Estate Act, No. 24 of 1913", seventy-four pages in length and implementing in-depth regulations that were an additional thirty pages long. The law required white estates to be centrally administered under the Master of the High Court. Native Estates, on the other hand, were governed by Section 18 of the "Native Administration Proclamation No. 15 of 1928", only two and a half pages in length. It was implemented through brief regulations that were published under Government Notice No. 70 of 1954, covering barely half a page. Native Estates were haphazardly administered by various decentralized structures across the Department of Native Administration and the Department of Justice.

This legislative bias against Native Estates resulted in inconsistent and confused administrative environments for Native Estates, contrary to white estates which were centrally administered under the Master of the High Court.

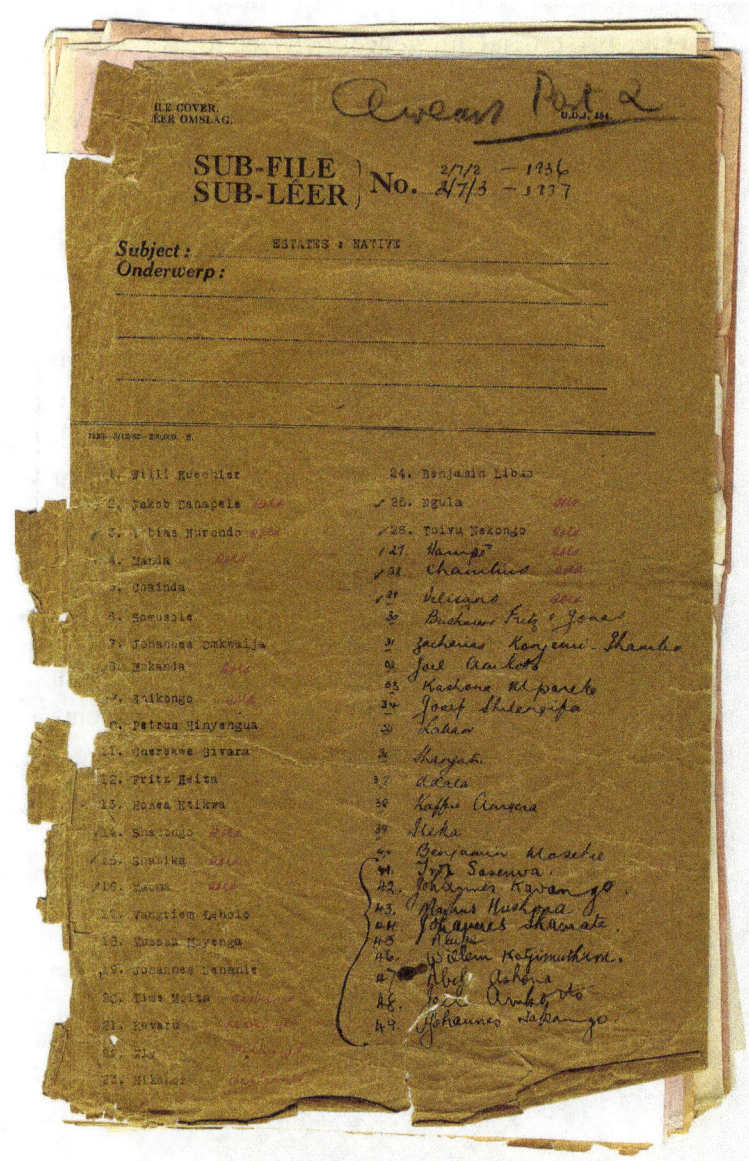

Figure 3: Cover of file. (NAN LGR [3/1/3] 2/7/3)

IDENTIFIED ESTATES

The investigation of the legal background lead to the conclusion, that Native Estates records must have been created. Further research revealed that they were indeed created, though haphazardly, and managed by Magistrates or Native Commissioners. Already the first of these records, once found, revealed that many offices falling under different authorities were involved in the day-to-day administrative processes of a native estate. However, there was no central office to collect, maintain and preserve all documentation of a single case. The surviving Native Estates records clearly show the signs of administrative neglect and chaos. It is not rare to find thirty cases crammed into one flimsy dilapidated file, arranged without any order (see Figure 3).

A systematic search through all relevant archival fonds of Magistrates and Native Commissioners eventually led to the discovery of 11 250 individual Native Estates case files at the NAN which had previously been believed to be lost or destroyed. The following tables (see Figures 4a, 4b) indicate the records that were found, arranged by the creating offices and on an annual basis. The tables reveal huge gaps in the Native Estates files in the Archives.

The table lists all record groups for which, according to legal provisions, one should expect estate files for the years 1916 to 1950. The black cells indicate the years where records were actually present. The huge gaps are obvious, as a large number of Native Estates records seem to have been destroyed, either by the creating offices or by the colonial archivists.

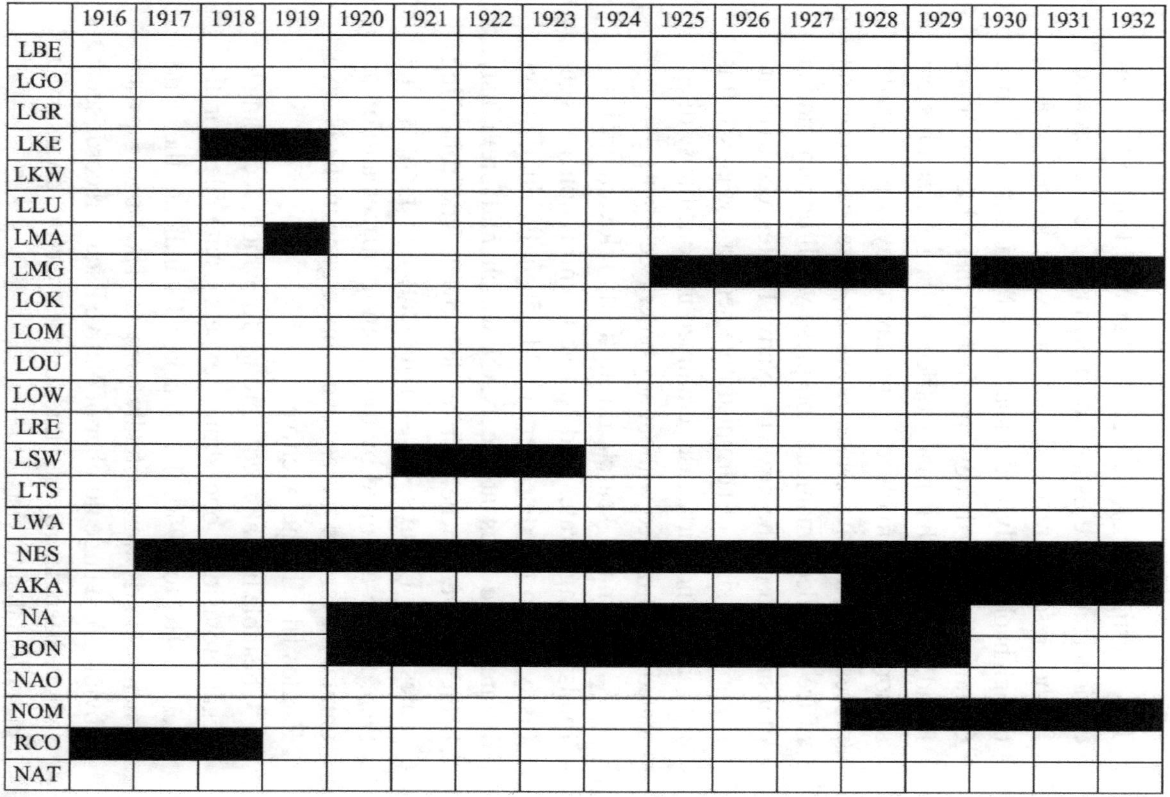

Figure 4a: Proven occurrences of Native Estates case files in the NAN (1916–1932) as per archival fonds.

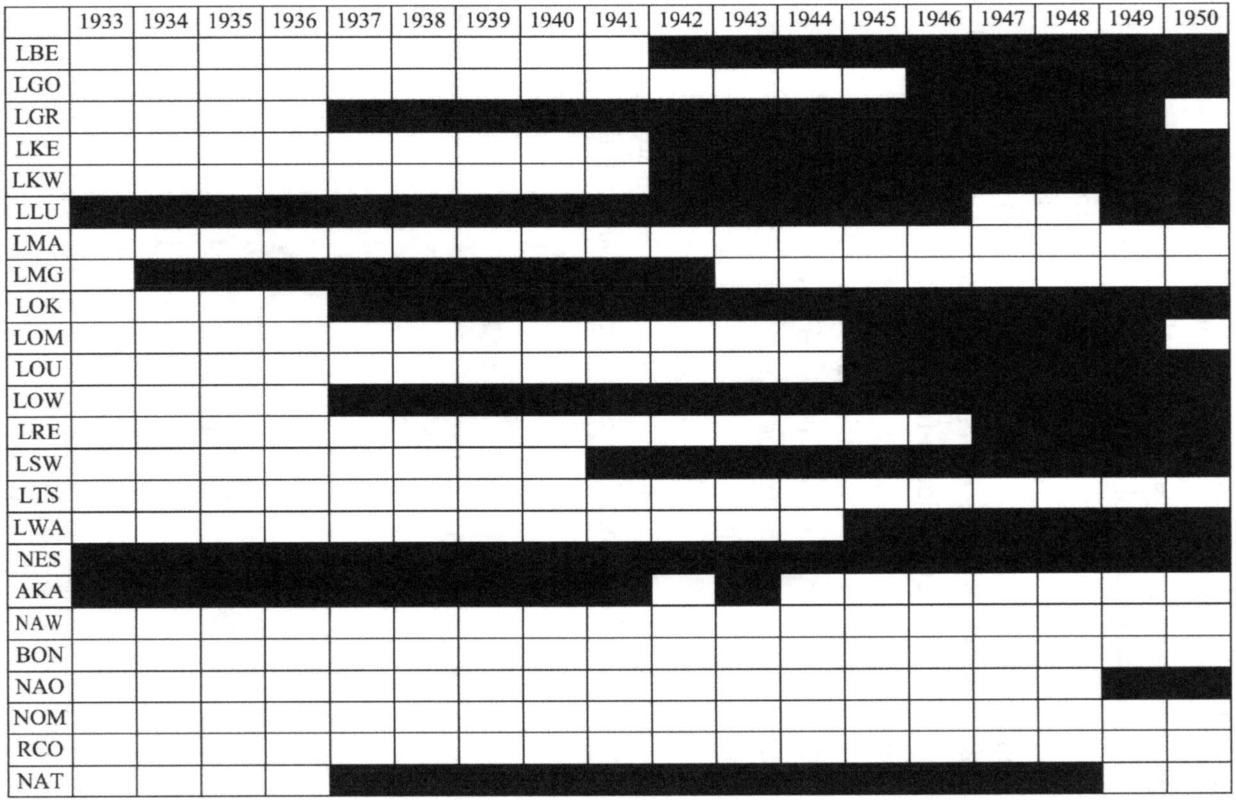

Figure 4b: Proven occurrences of Native Estates files in the NAN (1933–1950) as per archival fonds.

The following figure (see Figure 5) shows how many of the unexpectedly discovered 11 250 Native Estates files could actually be found with the help of the existing finding aids. About eleven per cent could be found by name in the electronic database, while an additional eight per cent was listed in (mostly handwritten) finding aids. The rest or eighty per cent were, for all practical purposes, completely hidden from the public view. One could call them "dark archives", in analogy to the "dark internet" that cannot be retrieved by search engines. Although physically present in the Archives, they were invisible to the retrieval tools and could neither be searched nor accessed.

An analysis of the content of the surviving Native Estates files shows that the vast majority deals with the

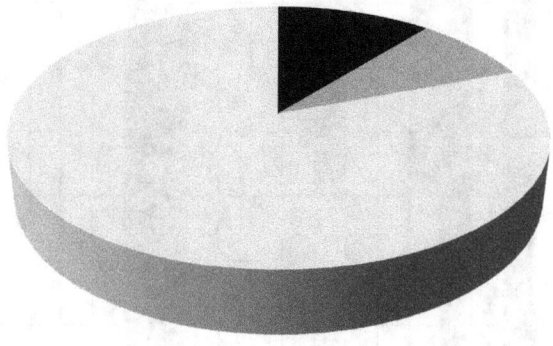

Figure 5: Accessibility of Native Estates files. Black: cases indexed in electronic database (10.9%); grey: cases indexed in hand-written finding aids only (8.8%); light grey: cases not captured in finding aids (80.3%).

estates of contract workers. As indicated in Figure 6, sixty-six per cent of the 11 250 discovered files belong to so-called "Northern Natives". These were men contracted from northern Namibia who died whilst working in the mines and other industries in southern and central Namibia. Upon their death the heirs had to be traced through chains of bureaucracies that included recruitment agents, traditional leaders, Magistrates, Native Commissioners and the police. Twenty-seven per cent of the discovered Native Estates case files belong to so-called "Extra-Territorial Natives" from other Southern and West African colonies and countries who died while working in various industries in Namibia. Only seven per cent of the files belong to "Local Natives", residents of central and southern Namibia and thus of the so-called "Police Zone".

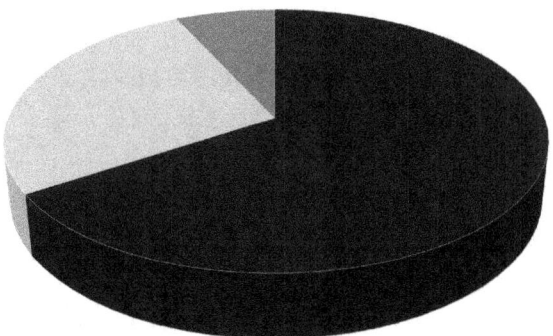

Figure 6: Composition of the Native Estates records population. Case files of Northern Natives Estates (black, 66%); Extra-Territorial Natives Estates (light grey, 27%), Local Natives Estates (grey, 7%).

At first view these figures seem surprising, considering that contract workers were at the bottom of the social ladder in terms of social standing, earnings, possessions, and social rights. However, the estates of the locally resident "Natives" were mostly dealt with according to customary law, by the family, and without interference by the state or the courts. Exceptions were those few cases where the monetary value of a local native estate exceeded the non-taxable amount. In this case the state took over its administration.

In the case of contract workers, whose families were living far away and not allowed to leave their so-called homeland, state structures were involved to ensure that the meagre possessions of the deceased were transferred to the inheritors. In cases were the inheritors could not be found, the proceeds from the sales of their estates were paid into the state coffers.

SURVIVAL, FORGETTING, AND REMEMBERING

Most of the gaps in the Native Estates records could not be adequately explained. They might have been destroyed at their offices of origin, or after appraisal at the Archives. From a few records in the NAN's own administrative files (the archives of the Archives) that deal with the actual destruction of Native Estates, it becomes clear that archivists during the apartheid era could not imagine any research use to emanate from Native Estates records and could not imagine insights

Figure 7: Typical users of the Archives during the colonial period. This illustration is taken from the Archives' pre-independence public relations brochure.

into the lives and deaths of "Natives" deriving from such records. Most appraisal recommendations by the archivists were made on the basis that Native Estates had no functional and no research value. Most Native Estates records discovered by this study escaped shredding or incineration only because they had never been appraised.

In contrast, the frequent use of white estate records by genealogists, for example, had prompted their meticulous preservation and indexing. The archivists' perception at the time of a typical user of the archive is strikingly illustrated by Figure 7.

More than half of the discovered Native Estates records belong to the record group NES (Native Estates), files created by the Chief Native Commissioner in Windhoek. This group, consisting of seventy-seven boxes with over 6000 case files, had been entirely forgotten and was only re-discovered in 2003 during a stocktaking exercise after the NAN had moved to new premises.

During my research I came upon correspondence between the archivist in Windhoek and his superior in Pretoria which revealed that these NES files were due to be destroyed in 1974. The Chief Archivist in Pretoria advised that
"The only value of these files lies in the presence of form NA16SWA: Death notice and particulars concerning the deceased. Please enquire about the registration of Bantu deaths by some authority in the territory before 1972 [...] the rest of the correspondence in the file apparently does not warrant permanent preservation. The decision about the value of the files will therefore depend on the results requested above and any further information that may be obtained on the duplication of the scanty genealogical information in the abovementioned form."[3]
The archivist in Windhoek could not find any other death registers, and this saved these estates from destruction—though not from being forgotten for the next thirty years. Work on a finding aid for the NES record group is mentioned once in the 1970s on an internal work plan but seems to have been abandoned without explanation in the following years. The fond was not even registered

in the *List of Archivalia* and therefore remained completely undiscoverable by researchers. In 2005 it was included for the first time in a new edition of the *List*.

AN UNDECIDABLE RESERVE

It is in the nature of formalized genres such as academic theses that one has to stick strictly to one's topic. Such restriction can be very frustrating to an author who, in the course of his or her work, stumbles across sources and topics that expand the narrow path set out by the agreed research questions.

This happened to me whilst conducting my research into the reasons why Native Estates files could not be found at the NAN. My research was not supposed to analyse the content of these files. Once these files (or rather, the surviving fraction) had been found, it was difficult to ignore the fact that they offered an untapped source for social history, especially for migrant labour history. It took the firm hand of my supervisor to prevent me from overloading my research with unrelated details of social history.

While it is uncertain whether my own workload will allow me to delve deeper into these issues, I would be glad if they were to be taken up in future research.

Migrant labour was a key feature in the social fabric of Namibia under colonialism. It runs like a "red thread" through the entire colonial period. As a central theme it interweaves with many strands of Namibian history and economy: racial discrimination, underdevelopment, resistance and the liberation struggle. It still has an impact on postcolonial social and political realities. There have been a number of academic studies on migrant labour in the Namibian context, most of them conducted before independence by critical scholars and at a time when understanding this feature was an important issue in supporting the liberation struggle.[4]

None of those studies could draw on the Native Estates records hidden away in the NAN and the details on thousands of individual workers who had died whilst in (and, as can be gleaned from the contents of many files, because of) the migrant labour system. Being hidden away in inaccessible files, nobody could expect that these records, apart from their genealogical value, would provide a glimpse into the harsh social realities of migrant labour.

In writing about archival ethics, the South African archivist Verne Harris postulates: "Legacies are never received; they are only ever made and re-made".[5] In this context, he cites Jacques Derrida:

"To inherit is not essentially to receive something, a given that one could then have. It is an active affirmation; it responds to an injunction, but it also presupposes an initiative, the signature, the countersignature of a critical selection. To inherit is to select, to sort, to highlight, to reactivate ... There is legacy only where assignations are multiple and contradictory, secret enough to defy interpretation, to carry the unlimited risk of active interpretation [...] A legacy must retain an undecidable reserve."[6]

Harris provides this quote in the context of discussing the legacy of Nelson Mandela. I think it resonates with the experience of colonial archives, of archives that were created to deal with a limited practical issue in the interest of the smooth administration of "the Native", but contain that *undecidable reserve* of unintended content, which needs to be actively interpreted. It is gratuitous that we have inherited these estate records, more by luck and neglect than by intention. It is up to us to reactivate them.

There is an emotional quality to dealing with these bureaucratic remnants of the lives of individuals, even though they predate us by one hundred years. Especially for me, as the daughter of a former migrant worker, it is difficult not to be touched when reading a death notice form that contains an exasperated side remark by a medical officer: *"this is the third native who died, out of six who walked in from the mine while suffering from pneumonia"*.[7] Such an unexpected outburst, suddenly revealing the human feelings of a colonial white man in the face of the inhuman treatment and suffering of a fellow black man at the hands of the management of the diamond mine, no matter how much he might have thought himself as superior to them, did certainly not carry the *"administrative value"* that the colonial archivist missed. And it certainly did not carry the type of *"research value"* the same archivist could imagine.

Likewise, the impression of reading the cause of death— "pneumonia"—in ten consecutive death notices for mine workers at the richest gem diamond mine in the world, in conjunction with their names and the few shillings of outstanding wages, gives a much stronger and indelible impression of their working conditions than a statistical table with the same information. This is one way how I understood the *"undecidable reserve"* of the archival legacy as highlighted by Derrida.

THE "EXTRA-TERRITORIALS"

The presence of a substantial number of "Extra-Territorial Natives" from outside the borders of colonial South West Africa was an unexpected result of my research. The details about their origin, possessions, marital status, cause of death etc. constitute a highly interesting and so far untapped source for the social history of inter-African migration. These details were not the subject of my study, which dealt solely with the presence or absence of Native Estates and the reasons thereof. As the actual content of the files warrants further research, some information should be presented here as a teaser to explore this resource in Namibia as well as possibly in South Africa and Zimbabwe where similar records might be found, although this has not yet been established. Exploring the online finding aids of South African archive depots reveals substantial holdings of Native Estates in the Cape Town and Pietermaritzburg repositories, but not in the former Transvaal where the vast majority of "extra-territorial" migrants worked. This does not mean that they do not exist—they might simply have been excluded from indexing just like it happened in Namibia.

The vast majority of "Extra-Territorials" in Namibia were migrant workers coming from Angola via the northern border. Their contracts were basically identical to those of the "Northern Natives". Most surprising was the substantial number of estate files from African migrants from other countries who had not come into Namibia under the standard contract labour system. This is a very diverse and heterogeneous group of people from all other Southern and Western African colonies. For this lecture I want to pick out details from two specific and prominent groups.

These are the West Africans, commonly referred to as "Kru boys", and the South Africans, commonly called "Cape boys", in the condescending colonial language which infantilised male adults into "boys".

The presence of West Africans in Namibia, especially Liberians, has long been known. They came mostly with short contracts to work as dock workers, already during the German colonial period, and sometimes stayed in the country. They were a cosmopolitan element which brought new and exciting ideas into the territory. In particular the Marcus Garvey Movement, which galvanized hopes of liberation in Namibia during the 1920s, showed a prominent involvement of West Africans, but very little else is known about these men and women.[8]

Even less is known about black South Africans—unskilled labourers as well as professionals such as teachers and nurses—who came to work in the territory that South Africa wanted to annex as its fifth province. With the exception of a few individuals who achieved political prominence, such as the nurse Putuse Appolus and the medical doctor Kenneth Abrahams, their presence went virtually unrecognised.

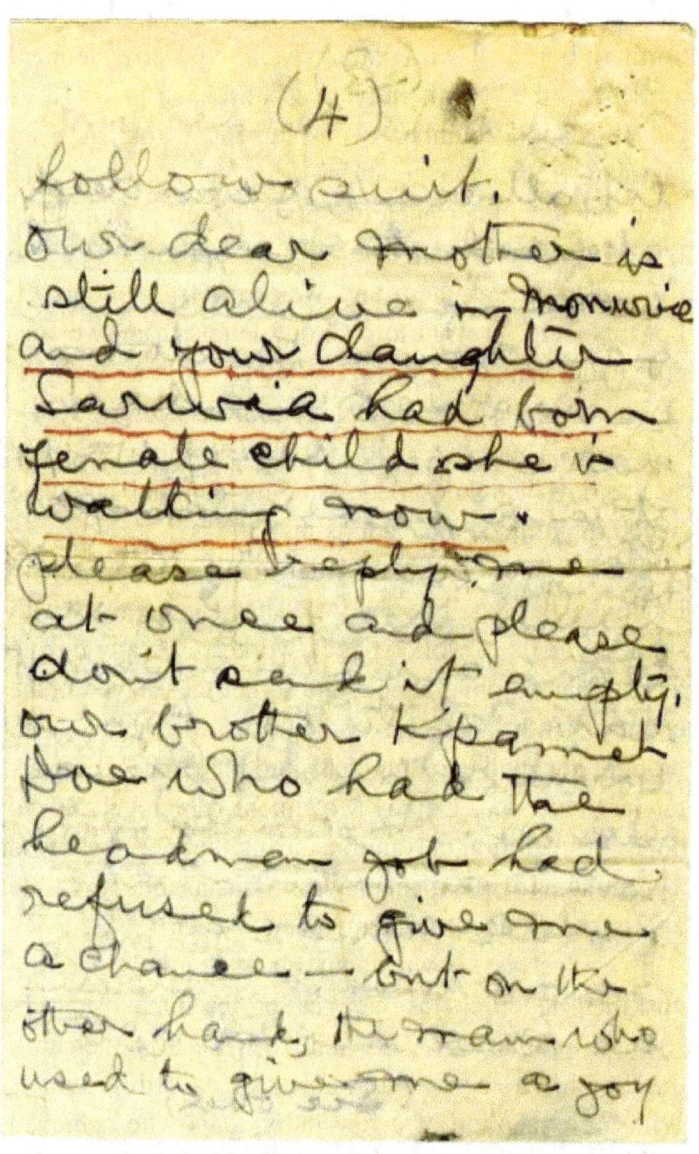

Figure 8 (left and right): "Our dear mother is still alive in Monrovia and your daughter […] born female child, she is walking now."
(NAN NES [3] 435 Estate Tom Glasgow)

(5)

had gone to prison x his name is Kpe Wree Minneh.

I am herewith sending you my photo and I wish you to send me your likeness too.

This leaves us all in good health.

I remain yours most sincere Brother

Teaplah Teah
alias Tom Glasgow.

Please bear in mind that if you want to send money then please send it to Sierra Leone and not to Monrovia.

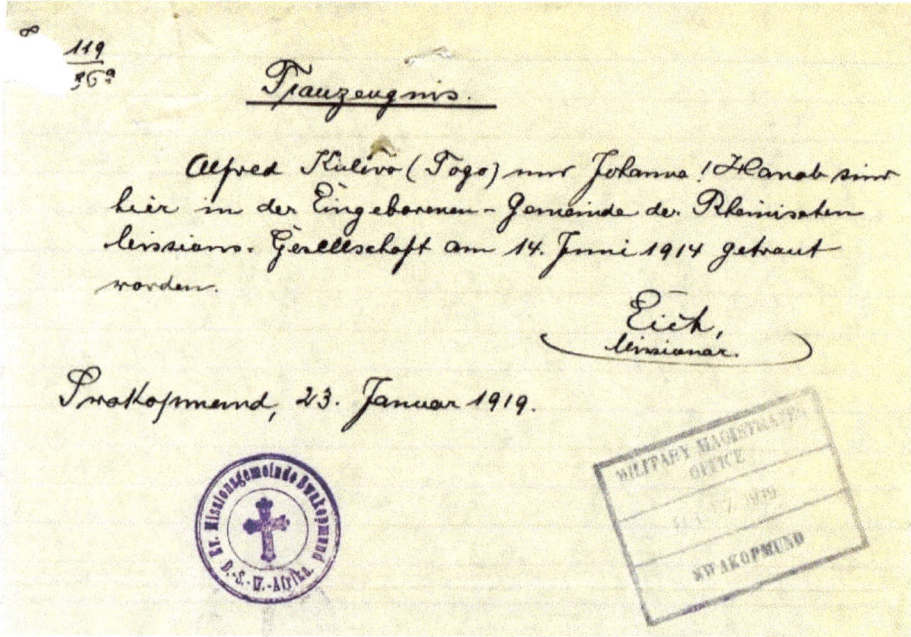

Figure 9: Marriage Certificate issued by the Rhenish Mission in Swakopmund for Alfred Kulivo from Togo and Johanna !Hanob. (NAN NES [4] 455 Estate Alfred Kulivo)

The estate papers of those who died on Namibian soil allow us to obtain a closer glimpse into their lives and their roots. Figure 8 shows an example of the rich genealogical value of such an estate file, which establishes the relationship between the deceased and potential inheritors.

A man in Sierra Leone writes to his brother in Lüderitzbucht. He mentions their mother in Liberia and the brother's daughter and grandchild, underlined in red. The record also documents a dual naming practice with

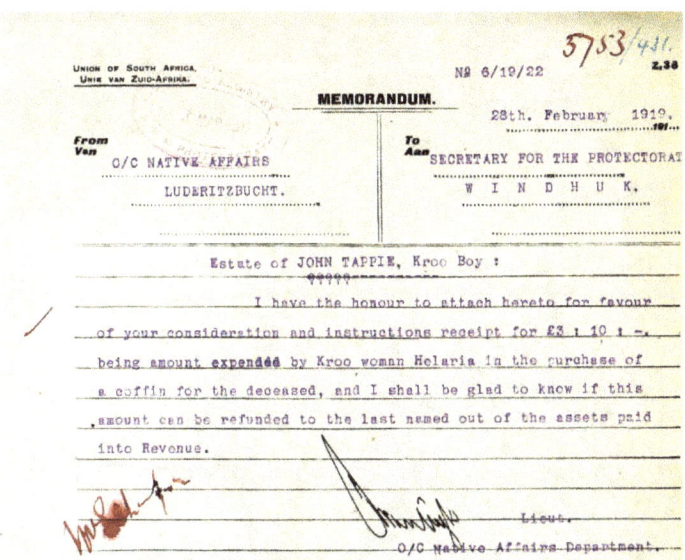

Figure 10: Cover note for a receipt of expenses incurred by a woman called Helaria from West Africa in the purchase of a coffin for a deceased fellow country man by name John Tappie.
(NAN NES [3] 431 Estate John Tappie)

the author using both the African name Teeplah Teah and the formal or Christian name Tom Glasgow—a key correlation for genealogical purposes which can, for example, link the person to an oral history which might only use the African name.

The estate papers also show marital ties with the local population, like a marriage certificate issued by a missionary who had performed the marriage between Alfred Kulivo from Togo in Swakopmund and Johanna !Hanob, obviously a local Damara woman (see Figure 9).

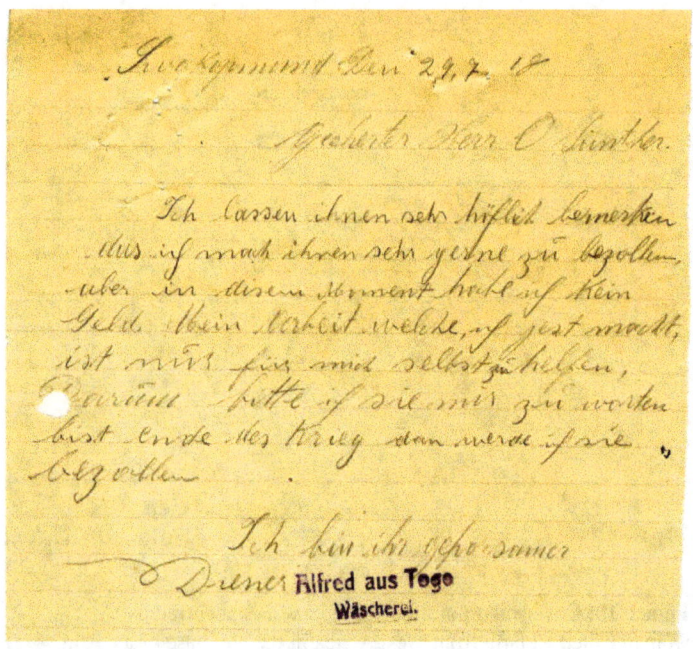

Figure 11: Letter by Alfred Kulivo from Togo asking for a respite for paying back his loan. (NAN NES [4] 455 Estate Alfred Kulivo)

Estate files also provide clues about ties of social solidarity within the expatriate West African community. Figure 10 demonstrates this kind of commitment by a woman who bought a coffin to provide a dignified memorial and burial service for a West African compatriot who had passed away. As it is certainly not common practice to spend money on buying a coffin for a deceased person with whom one is not biologically or matrimonially related, this memorandum demonstrates that there existed a cohesive community among the ex-

Figure 12: "Cape Boy" John Henry (left) standing on a locomotive he was working on. (NAN NES [6] 831 Estate John Henry Capeboy)

patriate West Africans beyond family ties. It also raises further questions: How did a woman from Liberia get to Namibia? What did she do for a living, being apparently independent enough to pay for a coffin? The migration of West African women to Namibia has never been mentioned, except in some cases as wives of deported Cameroonian soldiers.

Some records show entrepreneurial spirit in making a living in the foreign country, such as the already mentioned Alfred Kulivo from Togo. He established a laundry business in Swakopmund and bought a washing machine on credit but had to request for a respite when the First World War affected his business. When he died in the influenza pandemic of 1918, the unpaid sum was deducted from his estate (see Figure 11).

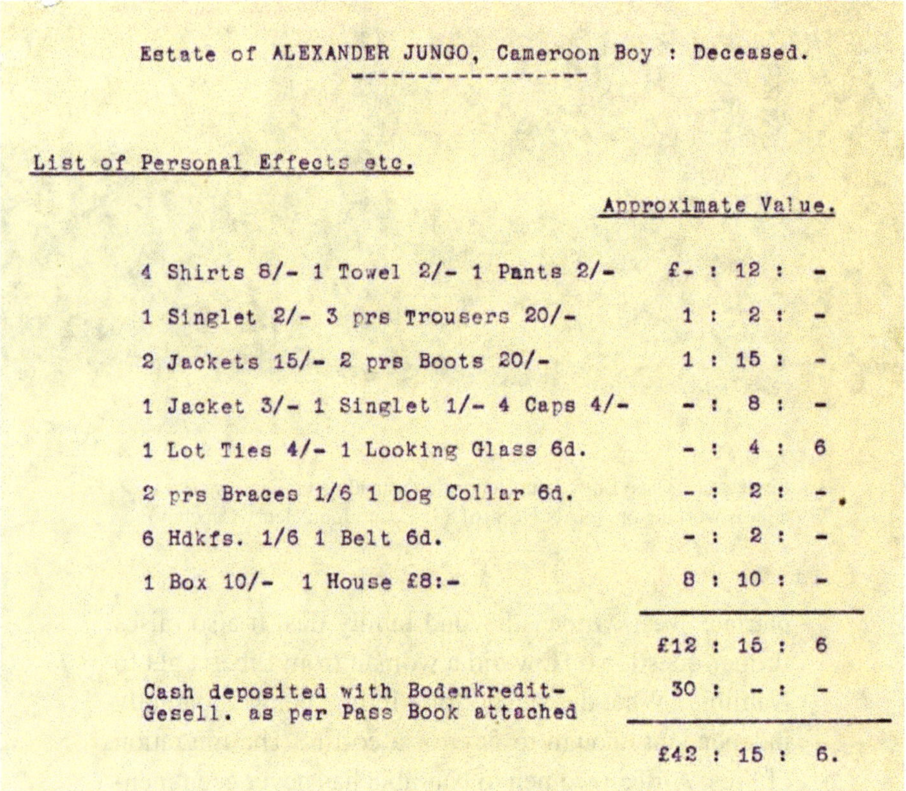

Estate of ALEXANDER JUNGO, Cameroon Boy : Deceased.

List of Personal Effects etc.

	Approximate Value
4 Shirts 8/– 1 Towel 2/– 1 Pants 2/–	£– : 12 : –
1 Singlet 2/– 3 prs Trousers 20/–	1 : 2 : –
2 Jackets 15/– 2 prs Boots 20/–	1 : 15 : –
1 Jacket 3/– 1 Singlet 1/– 4 Caps 4/–	– : 8 : –
1 Lot Ties 4/– 1 Looking Glass 6d.	– : 4 : 6
2 prs Braces 1/6 1 Dog Collar 6d.	– : 2 : –
6 Hdkfs. 1/6 1 Belt 6d.	– : 2 : –
1 Box 10/– 1 House £8:–	8 : 10 : –
	£12 : 15 : 6
Cash deposited with Bodenkredit-Gesell. as per Pass Book attached	30 : – : –
	£42 : 15 : 6.

Figure 13: The list of possessions of the late Alexander Jungu, a soldier from Cameroon documents, considerable wealth.
(NAN NES [3] 442 Estate Alexander Jungu)

Figure 14 (right): Declaration introducing the three brothers of the late Alexandre Nyongo (Alexander Jungu) as the rightful inheritors.
(NAN NES [3] 442 Estate Alexander Jungu)

CAMEROUN.

CIRCONSCRIPTION DE YAOUNDE.

CERTIFICAT D'HEREDITE.

L'An Mil Neuf Cent Vingt et Un, et le dix du Mois de Juin, Par devant Nous, RIPERT, Gaston, Administrateur des Colonies, Chef de la Circonscription de YAOUNDE, Chevalier de la Legion d'honneur, assisté de M.M. LE METAYER, Yves, Administrateur Adjoint des Colonies, Adjoint au Chef de l Circonscription de Yaoundé et DUBY, Raymond, Adjoint des Services Civils, Che de Subdivision de Yaoundé,

se sont présentés les nommés:

AMBOEMA MJOK, Chef de village, demeurant à NGETTE, race Sanaga;

BELINGA TCHO, Capitat, demeurant à NGETTE, race Sanaga;

MBA, Capitat, demeurant à NGETTE, race Sanaga;

ATEBA, Notable, demeurant à Ngette, race Sanaga;

ILONGO MBOELA, Notable demeurant à NGETTE, race Sanaga;

ETOKO AMBOEME, Notable, demeurant à NGETTE, race Sanaga;

BASSI MBOELE, Notable, demeurant à NGETTE, race Sanaga,

lequels, séparément et successivement, Nous ont declaré et certifié

que les seuls héritiers du nommé ALEXANDRE NYONGO, dit NYONGO BELIA, décédé à LUDERITZBUCHT (Sud-Ouest Africain) sont:

1o-ATEBA NOH, domicilié au village de NGETTE;

2o-BOKO MBOMBO, domicilié au village de NGETTE

3o-BENGALE, parti avec le de cujus au service des allemands, il y a dix ans environ et revenu dans son village à NGETTE;

que ces trois individus sont les frères consanguins du défunt Alexandre NYONGO;

qu'il n'existe d'autre part, tant du coté du père dudit NYONGO, que du coté de sa mère, actuellement tous deux décédés, aucun autre descendant:

enfin que les trois indigènes précités sont les seuls héritiers dudit NYONGO selon la coutume indigène formant Loi dans le pays.

En foi de quoi Nous avons dressé le présent certificat les jour, moi

The original administrative purpose of an estate file, namely to document how an estate was distributed or spent to cover outstanding debts, provides possibilities to capture such details of individual lives.

One can even find photographs, such as the one of "Cape Boy" John Henry, standing proudly on the locomotive he was working on (see Figure 12). The correspondence mentions that other photos from his estate had been sent to Cape Town by the Magistrate of Karibib in order to identify relatives as potential inheritors—unfortunately, in this case without success.

Some of the expatriates lived in Namibia for many years and saved money. Mr. Alexander Jungo or Jungu, a so-called "Cameroon boy", had a bank account to the value of £30, which was a lot of money during that time, especially for someone of his background (see Figure 13). He had been one of the Native soldiers in the German colony of Cameroon who were deported to Namibia in 1909 after a mutiny but continued to receive their salary.[9] Obviously, he must have saved his salary in the hope of returning home someday.

When his death was reported to Cameroon by the SWA Administration, the colonial authorities in Cameroon, which had meanwhile been taken over by France, established a carefully documented enquiry into the family and customary inheritance rules, and also established his real name Nyongo (see Figure 14).

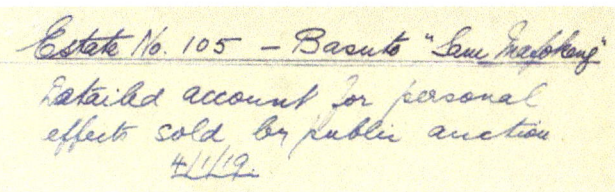

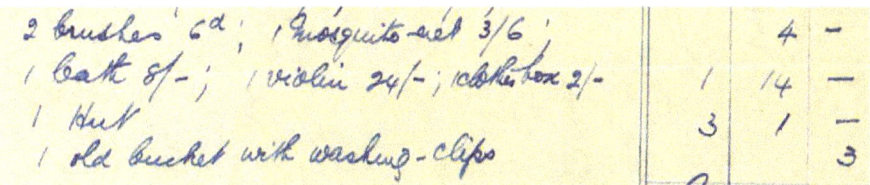

Figure 15: Among the possessions of the late Sam Mafokeng, a Basotho migrant worker at Lüderitzbucht, a violin features prominently. (NAN NES [3] 439 Estate Sam Mafokeng)

I want to conclude this overview of the research value of estate records with some facets from the estate inventories which also deserve further detailed analysis.

Musical instruments are surprisingly often present in the estate inventories of migrant workers who otherwise hardly owned more than the clothes on their bodies at the time of death. As is evident from the estate case file below, a Basotho migrant worker at the South African Railways in Lüderitzbucht owned a violin, and it is easy to imagine that he played it for weekend dances in the harbour town – although we would be very lucky indeed to find further evidence for that (see Figure 15).

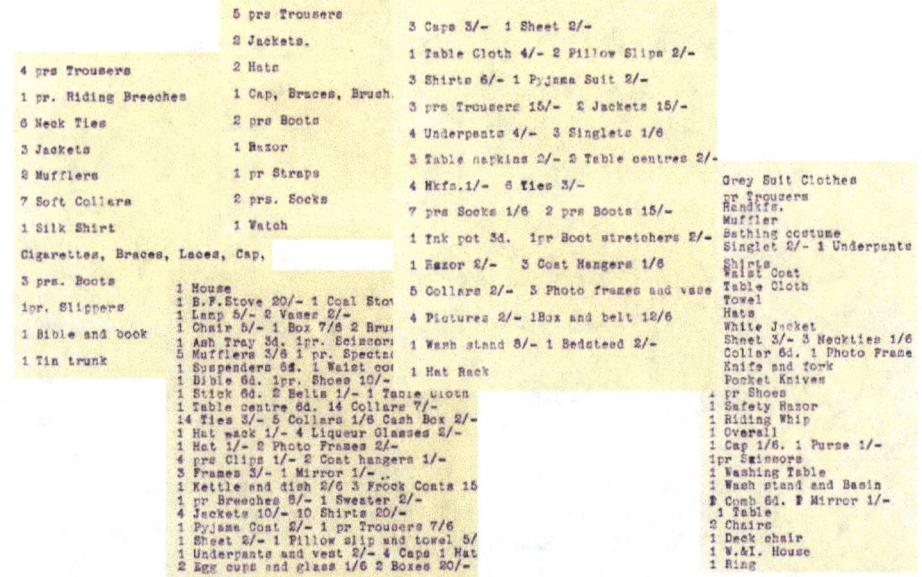

Figure 16: Clothing, accessories but also photo frames dominate the inventory of belongings of some deceased men from Liberia.
(Collage from various Native Estates files at the NAN)

The comparably better-paid or self-employed Liberians were obviously very concerned about their good looks, as is testified by their possession of neck ties, collars, silk shirts, and coat hangers. Unfortunately, one can only guess what pictures they would have displayed in their lodgings in the photo frames that are so frequently listed (see Figure 16).

OUTLOOK

I am happy to conclude this lecture with a recent fact that is not yet mentioned in my PhD-thesis as submitted. During July 2015, the NAN began to catalogue the NES records, and the first eight boxes containing 1 137 individual estate case files have to date already been entered into the database and are now accessible to the public. The data entry format has also been amended to take care of the issue of African names which do not fit Western naming conventions. In addition, the NAN has put the Native Estates on its priority list for digitisation.

Hopefully, these efforts will continue to cover all the over 11 000 Native Estates case files at the NAN, and open them up for family research as well as for academic social history.

ENDNOTES

1. Ellen Ndeshi Namhila: *The Price of Freedom*. Windhoek, 1997.
2. Ellen Ndeshi Namhila: *Kaxumba kaNdola. Man and Myth. The Biography of a Barefoot Soldier*. Basel, 2005.
3. NAN ARG [17] 10/1/2B Keuring van boedelrekords. Director of Archives to Chief Archivist, 2.8.1974.
4. Some of these critical authors are Lohmeier Angula, Gretchen Bauer, Robert Gordon, Richard Moorsom, Ndeutala Hishongwa, Susan Hurlich, Vitura Kavari, James Kauluma, John Loffler, Simon Zhu Mbako, Alastair McFarlane, Arthur Pickering, and Regina Strassegger.
5. Verne Harris: "Jacques Derrida meets Nelson Mandela: archival ethics at the endgame". *Archival Science,* Vol. 11, 2011, pp. 113–124, here p. 117.
6. Ibid. Harris cites from Jacques Derrida: *Negotiations: interventions and interviews 1971–2001*. Stanford, 2002, pp. 110–111.
7. NES [1] 135/105, Estate Rumingu. Captain J. B. Knobel from the Native Military Hospital on Shark Island, Lüderitzbucht (see Figure 1).
8. Gregory Alonso Pirio: *The Role of Garveyism in the Making of the Southern African Working Classes and Namibian Nationalism*. Los Angeles, 1982, unpublished paper (National Archives of Namibia).
9. NAN ZBU [0716] F.V., Kameruner Meuterer (1904–1914); see also Jan-Bart Gewald: "Mbadamassi of Lagos, a Soldier for King and Kaiser, and a Deportee to German Southwest-Africa". *Newsletter,* Namibia Scientific Society, Vol. 41, 2000, pp. 3–21, here p. 3.

CARL SCHLETTWEIN LECTURES

The distinguished lecture of the Centre for African Studies Basel is held in remembrance of Dr h.c. Carl Schlettwein, who played an important part in the development of African Studies at Basel and in the establishment of our Centre. His moral support was supplemented by the generous and farsighted assistance he gave to these activities. Carl Schlettwein was born in Mecklenburg in 1925 and emigrated to South Africa in 1952. Until 1963 he lived in South West Africa, the former German colony that was then under South African administration. When he married Daniela Gsell he moved to Basel. In 1971 Schlettwein founded the Basler Afrika Bibliographien (BAB) as a library and publishing house in order to allow international institutions to access bibliographic information on South West Africa (Namibia). Accordingly, he published the first national bibliography on this African country. Through these activities the BAB contributed to documenting and researching a nation with a particularly difficult history. Other publications dealt with historical, literary and geo-methodological topics, and included titles on Swiss-African relations. From an individualistic private initiative, the BAB developed into an institution open to the public and became a cornerstone of the Centre for African Studies Basel. As the Namibia Resource

Centre—Southern Africa Library the institution is of world-wide importance. The Carl Schlettwein Stiftung, which was founded in 1994, runs the BAB and supports students and projects in Namibia as well as in other Southern African countries. In 2001, the Carl Schlettwein Foundation funded the establishment of the Chair of African History, providing the basis for today's professorship in African History and the African Studies programme at the University of Basel. The Foundation works closely with the Centre for African Studies Basel to provide support for teaching and research and in 2016 it enabled the Centre to establish a position on Nambian and Southern African Studies. The University of Basel honoured Carl Schlettwein with an honorary doctorate in 1997.

www.ingramcontent.com/pod-product-compliance
Lightning Source LLC
Chambersburg PA
CBHW051544230426
43669CB00015B/2717